The Billion Dollar Saint

A FARCE IN THREE ACTS

⚜$⚜

By

Natalie E. White

DRAMATISTS PLAY SERVICE, INC.

To

Reverend Alfred F. Mendez, C.S.C.

The Billion Dollar Saint was first produced by the Department of Speech, University of Notre Dame, William J. Elsen, Head, for the Notre Dame Alumni Reunion on June 11, 1955 and for the Tenth Biennial Convention of the Catholic Theatre Conference on June 12th, with the folowing cast:

Father John Wickers, S.J., Professor at St. Ignatius_____Larry Rex

Brother Thomas, S.J., Sacristan and Porter of Loyola Hall_____John Kent

Father Philip Brooke, S.J., Vice President of St. Ignatius____Leonard Sommer

Gorboduc (Dutch) Jones, Star Tackle_____George O'Donnell

Saint Francis of Assisi_____Reginald Bain

Father Robert Lester, S.J., Vice President for
the Field of Studies_____James Carroll

Father Louis Cullen, S.J., Vice President for
Extra-Curricular Activities _____Taylor Benson

Father Francis of Assisi, O.F.M., Superior, Saint
Francis of Assisi Monastery_____Fred Syburg

Hank Hudson, Head Coach for Football_____Joe Boland

Mailman _____Larry Rex

Parcel Post Man _____James Kinnane

Milton Hoffman, Reporter and Photographer_____Sam Adelo

Professor Einsteider _____Michael Pap

John Stewart Owen, Secretary to the Secretary of State_____Leland Croghan

Michael Dunnovan, President of the Alumni Association_____William Elsen

Western Union Messenger _____Billy Elsen

The Football Team

The entire action of the play takes place in the outer office of the President of St. Ignatius University in Kansas. The time is the present.

ACT ONE
Friday, October 4th, about 7 A.M.

ACT TWO
Scene One: The Radio, Saturday, October 5th, about 4 P.M.
Scene Two: Monday, October 7th, about 10 A.M.

ACT THREE
Thursday, October 10th, about 3 P.M.

PRODUCTION
Director _____Fred Syburg
Set Design_____Rolland Stair, C.S.C.
Costume Design _____Jane Elsen
Stage Manager _____Hildegarde Vargyas

ACT ONE

[The scene is the outer office of the President of St. Ignatius University in Loyola Hall, the Administration Building. Up center, a little to the left, is a door leading to the hall; right is the door to the President's private office; on the left wall are two windows and from the view of the trees and other buildings outside we seem to be on the second floor. There are a desk and chair right, profile to the audience, and up left, a smaller desk, facing front. Pictures, religious and University, hang on the walls, and odd chairs and tables with University publications complete the furnishings.]

[It is Friday, October 4th, about 7:00 A.M.]

[BROTHER THOMAS, S.J., an elderly Brother, Sacristan of Loyola Hall Chapel and Porter of Loyola Hall, is seated behind the small desk, up center, obviously enjoying himself.]

[FATHER WICKERS, S.J., a young professor, is pacing up and down; he pauses left, and turns to Brother Thomas]

FR. WICKERS: If this is true, Brother Thomas, it is embarrassing to St. Ignatius University.

BR. THOMAS: It is true, Father Wickers.

FR. WICKERS: It's embarrassing to the whole Catholic Church.

BR. THOMAS: It's still true.

FR. WICKERS: He could be a clever imposter.

BR. THOMAS: He could be, but he's not.

FR. WICKERS: How do you know he's not?

BR. THOMAS: Father Wickers, I've told you: he's real. He's *Saint Francis*.

FR. WICKERS: If he's Saint Francis, why didn't he go to the Franciscans?

How do you account for his appearing to a Jesuit?

[5]

BR. THOMAS: Father, I've told you: he didn't "appear" to me; he is *not* an apparition.

FR. WICKERS: But what else could he . . .

[FATHER PHILIP BROOKE, S.J., First Vice President of St. Ignatius U., enters up center]

FR. WICKERS: Father Brooke!

FR. BROOKE: I came as quickly as I could. What's happened?

FR. WICKERS: Brother here has had an apparition.

BR. THOMAS: It was *not* an apparition.

FR. BROOKE: What did he see?

FR. WICKERS: He says he saw Saint Francis.

FR. BROOKE: Which Saint Francis?

FR. WICKERS: *Assisi.*

FR. BROOKE: Did you get me over here at this hour to try to tell me that with a Franciscan Monastery five miles up the road, St. Francis of Assisi has appeared to a Jesuit? — It doesn't make sense, Brother Thomas.

BR. THOMAS: I know it doesn't.

FR. BROOKE: Then why on earth have you gotten us over here with this absurd story?

BR. THOMAS: Father Brooke, I didn't *put* St. Francis of Assisi in the Chapel, I *found* him there.

FR. BROOKE: How do you know it was St. Francis of Assisi?

BR. THOMAS: He said so.

FR. BROOKE [after a moment's exasperated silence—to Father Wickers]: Have *you* been down to the Chapel?

FR. WICKERS: Not yet.

FR. BROOKE: And why not? The least you could have done was to check this ridiculous story before rousing the entire University.

BR. THOMAS: I'm afraid it's my fault—Saint Francis wanted to be left alone and I told him he wouldn't be disturbed.

FR. BROOKE: *You* told him?

BR. THOMAS: Yes, I did. — It was such a beautiful and rare thing to find a Saint praying in our Chapel, I made him welcome and invited him to stay. — What should I have done, Father Brooke?

FR. BROOKE: I don't believe your story, Brother. — Father Wickers, will you please go to the Chapel and if there *is* anyone there, apparition or imposter, tell him to come here, at once.

FR. WICKERS: Yes, Father Brooke. [Starts to door, u.c.]

[GORBODUC "Dutch" JONES, star tackle, enters, meeting Father Wickers. DUTCH is an amiable giant.]

DUTCH: Oh, Father Wickers, I was looking for you. — Father Brooke — Brother.

FR. WICKERS: I'm busy now — anything important, Dutch?

DUTCH: The football team is in the Chapel and there is nobody to say Mass.

FR. BROOKE: Our Chapel? Here in Loyola Hall?

DUTCH: Yes, Father.

FR. WICKERS: Did you notice — is there anybody in the Chapel?

DUTCH [puzzled]: Yes, Father: the football team.

FR. BROOKE: We know, we know — but anybody else?

FR. WICKERS: Was there anyone in the Chapel when the football team went in?

DUTCH: Nobody but a Franciscan.

FR. BROOKE: Oh, no!

FR. WICKERS: Was it a real Franciscan?

DUTCH: I thought they were all real.

FR. WICKERS: Did you notice anything unusual about him?

DUTCH: No, Father. I didn't pay any attention.

FR. BROOKE: Well, go right back and ask him to come here

DUTCH: The Franciscan?

FR. BROOKE: Yes.

DUTCH: All right, Father. [Starts to door u.c. and stops] Shall I tell him why?

FR. BROOKE: Just tell him to come.

DUTCH: O.K., Father. [Exit]

BR. THOMAS: As I said, Father, it's Francis himself.

FR. BROOKE: There are as many Franciscans named "Francis" as there are Franciscans and . . .

BR. THOMAS: But this is *Saint* Francis!

FR. BROOKE [Continuing] . . . and probably one stopped by from the Monastery. It's perfectly simple. All we have to do is explain that he is in the wrong—er—uh—

BR. THOMAS: — mansion?

[7]

FR. BROOKE: —chapel. — We can send him home in the President's car.

FR. WICKERS: That will be fine. Five miles is a long walk for a Franciscan. I don't see how they walk at all in those sandals.

BR. THOMAS: Saint Francis doesn't wear sandals. He's barefooted.

FR. BROOKE: All right, all right. Five miles is a long walk barefooted!

FR. WICKERS: There is an order of Franciscans that doesn't wear sandals.

BR. THOMAS: But they're in Canada. This is Kansas.

FR. WICKERS: You can get to Kansas quicker from Canada than you can from Assisi.

BR. THOMAS: Depends on *how* you travel.

FR. BROOKE: Father Wickers, will you get the President's car, please.

FR. WICKERS: The President is not in town — he won't be back till this afternoon. And he has his car with him.

FR. BROOKE: I thought he returned yesterday.

BR. THOMAS: He's not due back until the 4th — that's today — October 4th — the Feast of St. Francis.

[They look at him a moment]

FR. WICKERS: It could be some kind of joke.

BR. THOMAS: It could be, but it's not.

FR. BROOKE: Having a choice between believing that a Franciscan from a Monastery five miles away has appeared on the Feast of St. Francis to play a joke on a gullible Brother, and that St. Francis of Assisi has materialized in a Jesuit Chapel, I prefer to believe the joke. In fact, I . . .

DUTCH: [Returning quickly — He is barefooted!]: Father Brooke — the Franciscan will be up shortly; he preached a little sermon to the boys and now he wants to pray, and then he will come.

FR. BROOKE: Dutch! Where are your shoes?

DUTCH: I took them off, Father. *He* doesn't wear them when he talks to you, and it doesn't seem right to wear them when you listen. [EXIT]

BR. THOMAS: What were you saying about a joke, Father Brooke — before Dutch came back?

FR. BROOKE: This has gone far enough. Get the Franciscan Monastery on the phone.

FR. WICKERS: Their switchboard doesn't open for two hours.

FR. BROOKE: Then send them a telegram — there must be some way to reach them.

FR. WICKERS: Yes, Father Brooke. [Crosses to phone and begins to dial] If **he doesn't come** to us, we will have to go to the Chapel.

FR. BROOKE: It would be undignified to challenge a—

BR. THOMAS: — a saint?

FR. BROOKE: — a Franciscan — in the Chapel. It would seem inhospitable.

FR. WICKERS: Western Union? Will you take a wire please. It's to: Father Francis of Assisi, Superior, Saint Francis of Assisi Monastery, Saint Francis of Assisi, Kansas. — Just a moment — [to Fr. Brooke] What shall I say?

FR. BROOKE: Just tell him — uh —

FR. WICKERS: Yes?

FR. BROOKE: Just tell him the *truth!*

FR. WICKERS: Hello — Western Union? — just a moment — [to Fr. Brooke] How shall I word it?

BR. THOMAS: You could tell them there is in our Chapel a small, dark-haired saint, who says he is . . .

[SAINT FRANCIS OF ASSISI enters u.c. He looks very much as you would expect him to. He is small, with dark hair and dark eyes and a most expressive countenance. He is barefooted and his habit is ragged and torn].

ST. FRANCIS: Good morning, Fathers. I am Friar Francis and — Oh, good Brother Thomas, did you deliver my message?

BR. THOMAS: No, Saint Francis, I —

ST. FRANCIS [Holding up his hand gently]: "Friar" Francis — please.

BR. THOMAS: No, Friar Francis, they haven't given me a chance. Friar Francis, this is Father Brooke.

FR. BROOKE: I — I —

BR. THOMAS: And Father Wickers . . .

FR. WICKERS: Uh — good morning.

[FR. WICKERS, when he sees St. Francis, drops the phone on the desk — but not on the receiver. The phone clicks and clicks and you may even be able to hear the Western Union clerk's "Hello-hello" as he exasperatedly tries to make contact].

ST. FRANCIS: All I desire, Fathers, is to attend Mass in your Chapel. to sleep on your grass, and to preach God's love to the passerby. [There is a stunned silence] I can earn my keep. [Silence again].

BR. THOMAS: Well, Fathers, it's a modest request.

FR. BROOKE [Here is someone he can answer]: No.

ST. FRANCIS: No? — Then God's blessing on you — and I'll go my way. [Starts to door]

BR. THOMAS: Wait. [Turns to others] You know who he is — how can you let him leave?

[9]

FR. BROOKE: Have you any idea what will happen if he stays?

ST. FRANCIS: What Order is this?

BR. THOMAS: The Jesuit.

ST. FRANCIS: I do not know it. Who is your founder?

BR. THOMAS: St. Ignatius of Loyola — he's a later saint, Friar Francis — lived a few centuries after you.

ST. FRANCIS [Laughing]: You don't make much sense, good Brother Thomas. I am still alive — though transported miraculously to a strange place. [Walks to window left, and looks out] What is this land?

FR. WICKERS: Kansas

ST. FRANCIS: I never heard of it. — What are all these large buildings?

FR. BROOKE [He's just proud of his university]: This is St. Ignatius University, the finest Catholic school in the country — [pride struggles briefly with modesty, and wins] — probably the finest Catholic school in the world.

ST. FRANCIS: You teach from books?

FR. BROOKE: Yes — yes, we do. We endeavor, Frater, to inculcate in every student a love of learning, a great desire for knowledge, a . . .

ST . FRANCIS: Ah, Father! Consider this great desire of knowledge: have not all the great evils of the world come into the world through great desire of knowledge? Was it not through this that great Lucifer, Bearer of Light, fell and was cast out of Heaven? Through this great desire of knowledge was not our first parent, Adam, incited by this same Lucifer, driven from Paradise?

This great desire of knowledge, this pride of mind, this lifting up of the head in false learning — has it not brought to man all perils and all sufferings? And know you not instead that all good things that have ever come to pass in the world have come to pass through the abasement of the head, through the humility of this same mind?

Desire not knowledge! Desire rather holy humility, and to imitate pure simplicity and Our Lady Poverty. On these the first saints and friars did build. Humility should be your vocation — do not waste your time of living in vain and false study, lest you should find your hands empty in the day of tribulation — for, if you persist in the perilous pursuits of wisdom and knowledge you will be *confounded*.

Throw away *all books*, and turn away from all vain knowledge, and then you will find . . .

[DUTCH enters; still no shoes]

DUTCH: Brother Francis?

ST. FRANCIS: Yes, Big Little Brother Dutch?

DUTCH [to others]: Excuse me, Fathers. — Brother Francis, some more boys just came in the Chapel and would you please tell them what you said would happen to us if we go on reading books?

[10]

ST. FRANCIS: Gladly, Big Little Brother Dutch. [Starts toward door]

FR. BROOKE: Saint — Brother — Friar — please.

ST. FRANCIS: Excuse me, Father, I must go. [Exit, followed respectfully by DUTCH]

BR. THOMAS: Well, Father Brooke?

FR. BROOKE: Well what?

BR. THOMAS: Well, what are you going to do?

FR. BROOKE: I'm not going to do anything. I don't have to. [to Father Wickers] You said the President will be back today — he can handle it. That's why he's President — not just to give speeches at banquets. This is the President's job.

BR. THOMAS: Do you know where he is?

FR. BROOKE: Certainly, he's in Omaha.

[The PHONE begins to make long shrill noises — the Telephone Company is trying to attract the attention of whoever has left the receiver off the hook]

FR. BROOKE: Put the receiver on the hook, please. [Father Wickers does so]. Father Eddy should be in by two o'clock, maybe earlier.

[PHONE RINGS]

FR. BROOKE: Please answer it.

FR. WICKERS: Hello — hello — yes — he's right here. — It's for you. [Holds out phone to Fr. Brooke]

FR. BROOKE: [crossing to phone] Who is it?

FR. WICKERS: Long distance — Iona City.

FR. BROOKE: Who could be calling from Iona City?

FR. WICKERS: Probably the coach from Iona City University.

FR. BROOKE: The game's not till tomorrow — he couldn't be yelling "fake" already. Hello! Hello! [To others]: It's the President — it's Father Eddy. [In phone again] Hello, Hello, Operator, we have a bad connection. Please. All right. [Hangs up but keeps hand on phone] It couldn't be from Iona City because it's Father Eddy and he's in Omaha. [Phone rings and he answers immediately] Father Eddy? Yes, fine. I couldn't hear you before. It sounded as though you said you were in Iona City. — No! You said you would be back here today! — But the game isn't till tomorrow and Omaha is no closer to Iona City than it is to St. Ignatius.

Father Eddy — look — I don't want to talk on the phone, but something has happened — something very strange — don't make me tell you, just come back at once. — You can fly home this morning and fly back for the game tomorrow. — I know you haven't seen a game this season, but you're not a Freshman. — I *can't* tell you what the trouble is; you've got to take

[11]

·ny word for it and come back. — Of course I can handle anything within reason and so can the other three vice-presidents, but this isn't within reason. —

All right: Brother Thomas found St. Francis of Assisi in the Chapel. — I am serious. — What? — Yes, I said Mass at 6:15. Why? — Father Eddy! Wait!— You don't understand — Operator — operator — we've been cut off — [Slams receiver down].

FR. WICKERS: What did he say?

FR. BROOKE: He said to go light on the wine.

BR. THOMAS: That settles everything.

FR. WICKERS: What will you do?

FR. BROOKE: I'll call in the other Vice Presidents — that's what I'll do. Let them handle it.

BR. THOMAS: But you're First Vice President — it's your job.

FR. BROOKE: Not necessarily. It seems to me from what the Saint said about books, it's a matter for the *Second* Vice President, for the vice president in charge of the Field of Studies — that's it: The Field of Studies. [He crosses to phone as he talks and dials an extension]. Father Lester wouldn't like me to interfere — [On Phone]: Hello, Bob? — Fine — and you? — Bob, we have a little problem over here that comes under your jurisdiction and I think you will want to handle it yourself. — We're in the President's office. — We'll wait for you. — O.K. [Hangs up].

FR. WICKERS: What do you think he'll do?

FR. BROOKE: That's going to be his problem, and I'm not going to influence him. He can handle the entire matter any way he sees fit.

FR. WICKERS: I have an idea. [Fr. Brooke looks at him sharply and he continues somewhat apologetically] It may not be a good idea — but if we could send someone over to the Franciscan Monastery and ask Father Francis, the Superior of the Monastery, to come here — we could then — *introduce* him to the Saint — and — well —

FR. BROOKE: — he might take him off our hands!

BR. THOMAS: You'll never get him over here.

FR. BROOKE: Why not?

BR. THOMAS: He'll be too busy celebrating his Feast Day.

FR. BROOKE: Have *you* any idea how we could proceed?

BR. THOMAS: No. And I'm enjoying the situation just as it is.

FR. BROOKE: Father Wickers, it was your idea. Take a taxi and go on over there.

FR. WICKERS: I didn't have myself in mind. I wouldn't know what to say.

FR. BROOKE: It doesn't matter what you say — just bring Father Francis back.

[12]

FR. WICKERS: I have to say *something*. I can't kidnap him.

FR. BROOKE: Tell him we have a *special surprise* for his Feast Day. Extend the invitation in the President's name — in his absence. Take the black limousine

BR. THOMAS: He'll think it's a funeral.

FR. WICKERS: How do you know it will run? It hasn't been out since the last Cardinal was here. [Starts to the door and turns] I feel conspicuous driving that black limousine down the highway.

FR. BROOKE: Nonsense.

FR. WICKERS: It isn't nonsense. All the convertibles genuflect to it.

[FATHER LESTER enters. He is Second Vice President, in charge of the Field of Studies]

FR. LESTER: Good morning, men. — Brother Thomas.

BR. THOMAS: Good morning, Father Lester.

OTHERS: Good morning.

FR. LESTER [For some reason he is in a good mood]: Now, what is this *little problem* you want me to take over?

[There is a silence. Father Brooke doesn't know how to begin].

FR. WICKERS: Well, I guess I'll get along. I'll be back soon — probably. [EXITS]

FR. LESTER: Where is Father Wickers off to?

BR. THOMAS: The Franciscan Monastery.

FR. LESTER: At this hour?

FR. BROOKE: We have a little surprise for their Feast Day.

BR. THOMAS: It isn't particularly "little."

FR. LESTER: Am I supposed to ask whether Father Wicker's journey has anything to do with the little matter you wanted to talk over with me?

BR. THOMAS: It has.

FR. BROOKE: Yes — er . . . Oh! What's the use!

FR. LESTER [Jokingly]: If one of the football players has flunked a test I can't do a thing.

FR. BROOKE: This is serious.

FR. LESTER [still joking]: More serious than football in October?

FR. BROOKE: Briefly, Bob — and don't tell me you don't believe me — Saint Francis of Assisi has appeared on our campus.

FR. LESTER: Are you joking?

FR. BROOKE: No.

[13]

FR. LESTER: When did he appear?

BR. THOMAS: This morning — about 6:30.

FR. LESTER: Who saw him?

FR. BROOKE: Brother Thomas

BR. THOMAS: I did   (Simultaneously)

FR. LESTER: Where was he?

BR. THOMAS: Right downstairs in the Chapel.

FR. LESTER: It's simple: just don't say anything about it, Brother Thomas, until we can have an investigation — privately. A personal revelation does not have to be broadcast. — Brother Thomas — would you — 'er — wait outside a moment?

BR. THOMAS: I'd rather listen.

FR. BROOKE: Bob, I don't think you . . .

FR. LESTER: Please.

BR. THOMAS [x to door]: All right — but you're going to be surprised. [EXIT]

FR. LESTER: Now, really, Brother Thomas is old, and if he starts "seeing saints" . . .

FR. BROOKE: Bob, sit down.

FR. LESTER: What?

FR. BROOKE: Sit down. — I hate to tell you this, but we are all "seeing saints."

FR. LESTER: You mean, *you* have seen him too?

FR. BROOKE: Yes. I have seen him and I believe him. That is: I believe he's St. Francis. I don't believe what he says, of course. He's very Franciscan.

FR. LESTER: Well, this puts it in a different light. But we should be able to keep it quiet. That's the main thing: Keep it quiet. You know, this kind of thing won't be believed.

FR. BROOKE: That had occurred to me.

FR. LESTER: You realize, this doesn't make sense.

FR. BROOKE: That's why I called you.

FR. LESTER: Wait a minute . . .

FR. BROOKE: I don't mean it that way. — St. Francis is preaching against worldly learning — against books — he is talking to the students about the evils of . . .

FR. LESTER: Did you say students?

FR. BROOKE: Yes. Why?

[14]

FR. LESTER: He is giving lectures to the students?

FR. BROOKE: Yes.

FR. LESTER: Addressing them outside of the classrooms — on the campus?

FR. BROOKE: Yes.

FR. LESTER: The solution is simple; this is not a matter for the Field of Studies. All lectures, speeches and entertainments are Extra-Curricular Activities and the Vice President in Charge of Extra-Curricular Activities should handle it. I will turn it over to Father Cullen [crosses to phone]. You had no business calling me in on this, Phil; you know I never interfere with another Vice President. [Dials]

FR. BROOKE: But, Bob, if you had seen the Saint — and heard him . . .

FR. LESTER: He's not in his room. [Dials again] I'll try his office.

FR. BROOKE: Before you get him . . .

FR. LESTER [Hanging up]:   He's not at the office. [Pacing] It's almost 8 o'clock — where would he be? He's said Mass and had breakfast and . . .

[FATHER LOUIS CULLEN, S.J. enters. He is Vice President in Charge of Extra Curricular Activities]

FR. CULLEN: Good morning, Phil — Bob — I . . .

FR. LESTER: Louis! We were just trying to get you.

FR. CULLEN: What's Brother Thomas laughing about? When he saw me he started roaring and said: "Three down and one to go." — Is this a meeting of Vice Presidents?

FR. BROOKE: In a way.

FR. CULLEN: Well, let's get it over with fast.

FR. LESTER: Louis, we've got a problem on our hands.

FR. CULLEN: In what way is Extra-Curricular Activities involved?

FR. BROOKE: We have an unscheduled — lecturer — on the campus.

FR. CULLEN: I'll get him off. Where is he?

FR. LESTER: Downstairs in the Chapel.

FR. CULLEN: In the Chapel here! [Starts to door] I'll put a stop to that. [Turns back] What's his name?

FR. BROOKE: Saint Francis of Assisi.

FR. CULLEN: I don't care if it's Saint — [pause; then walks d.c. slowly] What did you say?

FR. LESTER: He said: Saint Francis of Assisi.

FR. CULLEN: Have you seen him?

FR. BROOKE: I have.

[15]

FR. CULLEN: Where is he from?

FR. BROOKE: Assisi — via Heaven, we presume. [Laughs feebly].

FR. CULLEN: Are you pulling a joke — or is this something the Franciscans have rigged up?

FR. BROOKE: Look, Louis, we've heard the man — he's real. No Franciscan has spoken like that since the first one.

FR. CULLEN: But this could be embarrassing.

[Father Brooke and Father Lester laugh a little bitterly]

FR. BROOKE: That's why we called you in.

FR. CULLEN: Why me? — Hey, where's the President? — If it's this big, the President should handle it himself. What does he think he's President for?

FR. BROOKE: To go to football games. — I've had a call from him and he's in Iona City, waiting for the game to start tomorrow.

FR. CULLEN: Didn't you explain to him?

FR. BROOKE: Of course I did.

FR. CULLEN: What did he say?

FR. BROOKE: Never mind.

FR. CULLEN: He didn't believe you?

FR. BROOKE: That's right.

FR. CULLEN [slowly]: Thinking it over, neither do I.

[DUTCH enters again, a little breathless]

DUTCH: Excuse me, Father Brooke, I don't want to interrupt you but . . .

FR. CULLEN: Gorboduc Jones! Where are your shoes?!!

DUTCH: Father! You promised you'd never call me *Gorboduc!*

FR. CULLEN: I never expected to see a St. Ignatius boy with his shoes off. Put them on, at once!

DUTCH: But Father Cullen, I . . .

FR. CULLEN: At once! Don't argue.

FR. BROOKE: Just a moment, Father Louis. — Dutch, where is St. Francis?

DUTCH: Gee, Father, that's what I wanted to tell you. There are so many boys trying to get into the Chapel we thought maybe if we got the Assembly Hall *everybody* could hear the Saint.

FR. BROOKE: *Everybody!* No. Of course you can't have the Assembly Hall — this whole situation is unprecedented and — I'm sorry. I'm sorry. I'm speaking out of turn. I forgot. — Father Cullen is in charge of extracurricular activities; talk to him.

[16]

DUTCH: Well — O.K. — We just want the Hall for a little ᵥ
Cullen.

FR. CULLEN: Let me think about it.

DUTCH: An hour is all we want it.

FR. BROOKE: Dutch, why don't you take the Saint out and get
breakfast? He must be tired, talking all this time.

DUTCH: I don't think he'll want to stop, Father.

FR. LESTER: We should show him St. Ignatius hospitality.

FR. BROOKE: He might even want to lie down for a while.

FR. LESTER: Yes. If we could just get him to lie down and rest and
quiet.

DUTCH: Oh, Father, he's got lots of energy; he could go on all day.

FR. BROOKE: Oh, no.

DUTCH: He's sharp; he's on the ball. — Is he really a saint?

FR. BROOKE: He didn't say so.

DUTCH: I've never seen a saint before and he sure is different from what
I expected. Everything he says makes sense.

FR. LESTER: He's a saint.

DUTCH: Say! Why couldn't we take him to the game with us? He's probably never been in an airplane.

FR. BROOKE: He's been flying around for years.

DUTCH: Well what about the Assembly Hall? We don't have much time
because the team's got to catch the plane at 10 o'clock.

FR. LESTER: Ten o'clock! It's almost eight now. You've got to get breakfast and pack and . . .

DUTCH: But, Father, it won't take long to . . .

FR. BROOKE: Dutch! Stop arguing and be on your way. You'll be late
and you know how easily the Coach gets upset.

DUTCH: I know, Father. He's tired.

FR. LESTER: And don't let him see you with your shoes off.

DUTCH: But, Father . . .

FR. CULLEN: Dutch, you know we're worried about the Coach. He's a
nervous man. We must all cooperate and keep him calm. No excitement.

DUTCH: Yes, Coach. — Father.

FR. BROOKE [raising voice]: And you get out of here!

DUTCH [Swings around to leave]: Yes, Father!

[17]

FR. LESTER: Why should he be overlooked?

FR. BROOKE: He's as much a vice-president as we are.

FR. CULLEN [Dialing]:   You know, I sometimes wonder if we have too many vice-presidents. — He's not in his room; I'll try the refectory. [Dials again].

FR. LESTER: He should be through eating.

FR. CULLEN: Hello — this is Father Cullen. Is Father Sullivan there? — Father Jim Sullivan. — Tell him it's important. [To others]: He's there.

FR. LESTER.   Tell him to come on over.

FR. BROOKE: Tell him we'll wait for him.

FR. CULLEN: Hello, Jim. Phil and Bob and I are in the President's Office and we want you to join us and . . . What? — No, we were not going to try to palm off St. Francis on Business Administration! — What? — You can't go to Iona City today. — The football team has one chaplain, that's enough! — They don't *all* have to go to Confession to beat Iona! — No! — Jim, listen! [Hangs up]).

FR. BROOKE: Well, that was hilarious.

FR. LESTER: How did he know about it?

FR. CULLEN: It must be getting around the campus.

FR. BROOKE: That brings us back to what do we do about the Saint.

FR. LESTER: Should we call the Bishop?

FR. BROOKE: If you want to, go ahead. [Very Fast] But don't ask *me* what to say to him.

FR. CULLEN: What could the Bishop do?

FR. BROOKE: Get in touch with the Archbishop.

FR. CULLEN: And the Archbishop could . . .

FR. BROOKE: Stop right there!

[BROTHER THOMAS enters]

BR. THOMAS: Excuse me — Father Wickers is returning with a Franciscan, a Twentieth Century Franciscan, and could I watch?

FR. BROOKE: Brother Thomas, your attitude toward this phenomenon is lacking in proper spirit.

BR. THOMAS: Since I discovered the "phenomenon" I thought I could regard it in any spirit I liked.

[Enter FATHER WICKERS and FATHER FRANCIS OF ASSISI. FATHER FRANCIS is a large man, ordinarily amiable, and, as befits the Superior of an Order, forceful in bearing; but right now his amiability has been subjected to a hard test and he is verging on outright irritability. He wears sandals.]

[19]

FR. BROOKE: Father Francis! We *are* glad to see you and it was good of you . . .

FR. FRANCIS: Father Brooke —you sent for me. Would you mind telling me why?

FR. BROOKE: Didn't Father Wickers tell you?

FR. WICKERS: Not exactly — I — er [a sudden inspiration] I knew you could explain it so much better [gets a withering glance from Father Brooke and continues falteringly] and — I thought I would — just — let *you* do it.

FR. BROOKE: I'd rather *you* did.

FR. WICKERS: Well — I — uh — excuse me — just thought of something — excuse me. [EXIT]

FR. FRANCIS: Fathers, I am a busy man — nothing could have persuaded me to come here on the Feast Day of Blessed Saint Francis except that black limousine. When Father Wickers drove up in that hearse I knew somebody had died, or a Cardinal had come — which is it?

FR. BROOKE: Father Francis, wouldn't you like to sit down?

FR. FRANCIS: No.

FR. CULLEN: Would you care for some coffee?

FR. FRANCIS: No.

FR. LESTER: It's a lovely morning.

FR. FRANCIS: It was.

[There is a silence]

FR. FRANCIS: Fathers, you are all acting very strangely, and I suppose I should be curious, but I'm not. Whatever has happened, Fathers, you can tell me about it some other time. [Starting to the door] I am now returning to the Monastery to continue the ceremonies for the Feast of Our Blessed Saint Francis.

FR. BROOKE: Why don't you continue them right here?

FR. FRANCIS: Continue devotions to Saint Francis in a Jesuit University? What would St. Francis think?

BR. THOMAS: Why don't you ask him? [Father Francis looks at him] He's in the Assembly Hall, talking to the students.

FR. CULLEN: How did he get in the Assembly Hall?

FR. LESTER: Who let him in there?

BR. THOMAS: I opened it for him.

FR. BROOKE: You? Who gave you permission?

BR. THOMAS: I didn't think I needed any.

FR. BROOKE: So you *presumed* to . . .

BR. THOMAS: I didn't presume anything. I just put the Saint in the Assembly Hall.

FR. FRANCIS [Who has been looking from one to another in bewilderment]: Fathers, I know I am only a guest here, but would you mind telling me what you are talking about? *Who* you are talking about?

BR. THOMAS: The Saint — Saint Francis of Assisi, the first. He appeared in our Chapel this morning and has been preaching to us ever since. Everybody loves him — at least the boys do.

FR. FRANCIS: Is this a joke?

FR. CULLEN: No. It just sounds like one.

FR. FRANCIS: How long has he been here?

FR. LESTER: Since 6:30.

FR. FRANCIS: What does he look like?

BR. THOMAS: Well — he's barefooted and poorly dressed and . . .

FR. FRANCIS: Some kind of fanatic! — What made you think he was the Saint?

BR. THOMAS: He *said* he was.

FR. FRANCIS: Anybody could *say* he was Saint Francis of Assisi — I could say I was the Pope. Did you *question* him?

FR. BROOKE: No, we didn't.

FR. FRANCIS: Why didn't you question him?

FR. CULLEN: It didn't occur to us.

FR. FRANCIS: Obviously the first thing we have to do is call him in here and question him. Where did he come from? How did he get here? Bring him in; I'll question him.

BR. THOMAS: Father! He's not Bernadette.

FR. FRANCIS: Well, whoever he is, he's an imposter.

FR. LESTER: You haven't seen him or heard him — you don't know.

FR. CULLEN: Wait till you hear him speak.

FR. BROOKE: There is no doubt whatever in our minds that he is who he says he is: Saint Francis of Assisi.

FR. FRANCIS [After looking at them each and all carefully and detecting no trace of a joke, he speaks slowly]: If he really is the Saint, which all of you seem to believe [Speaks rapidly] What are you doing with him here? Why don't you return him to the Franciscans where he belongs? Think what a laughing stock it will make of us if it is discovered that our own Saint passed us by while we were celebrating his feast to appear to some Jesuits. This is ridiculous! I demand that you turn St. Francis over to me at once.

[There is a contented silence from the Jesuits: they proceed cautiously, not wanting to exchange glances or appear happy too soon]

FR. BROOKE: We aren't sure that is the proper way to proceed — there is no precedent and . . .

FR. FRANCIS: There is only one way you can proceed — release the Saint.

FR. CULLEN: Perhaps we ought to consider it a while.

FR. LESTER: After all, he did appear to us.

FR. BROOKE: We don't want to seem inhospitable to him.

FR. CULLEN: Absolutely not.

FR. LESTER: But if you *insist*—

FR. FRANCIS: I *do* insist.

FR. BROOKE: In that case — we are close neighbors and we don't want to do anything to cause friction between the Franciscans and the Jesuits.

FR. CULLEN: Would you like me to take you to the Assembly Hall?

FR. LESTER [Warningly]: Maybe it would be better to bring the Saint to Father — the Assembly Hall is crowded — might be difficult to — er —

FR. BROOKE: You are *right!* Father, you stay here and I'll send . . .

COACH'S VOICE [offstage]: WHERE ARE THEY? WHERE'S THAT TEAM?

FR. CULLEN [backing from door]: It's the Coach. It's Hank Hudson.

FR. LESTER [also backing instinctively]: Oh — oh. Stormy weather.

COACH'S VOICE [offstage]: I WANT THAT TEAM!

FR. BROOKE: Brace yourselves.

[COACH HANK HUDSON enters stormily. The Coach is not old in years, but football wears a man down; still the top coach in the country and winning every game, his nerves are completely shot.]

COACH [Shouting]: WHERE'S MY FOOTBALL TEAM!

FR. BROOKE: Wait a minute, Coach, don't get upset.

COACH: If anyone else tells me not to get upset this season I am going to resign. I'm going to resign if its 4th down, 4th quarter, four seconds to go and four referees on the other side! I CAN'T FIND MY FOOTBALL TEAM!

FR. BROOKE: It's *all right*, Hank.

COACH: It's not all right. They're not in the dining hall and they're not in their rooms. They haven't had breakfast and they havn't packed. Where are they and what are they doing? We've got the toughest game of the season tomorrow and I can't find the team.

[22]

FR. BROOKE: Coach! Please! We have company. This is Father Francis of Assisi.

COACH [taken aback]: Oh!

FR. BROOKE: He is Superior of the Franciscan Monastery — our neighbor — our next-door neighbor — [laughs and others join] — our good neighbor.

COACH: I'm glad to meet you, Father. You were all so solemn I thought for a moment I was being introduced to the Saint. [Laughs — alone].

FR. LESTER: No. This is not Saint Francis — that is, not the — I mean: he isn't.

COACH: I am glad of it.

BR. THOMAS: St. Francis is much smaller.

COACH [to Jesuits]: Now, if you will just help me find my team — the plane leaves shortly and I'VE GOT TO HAVE MY FOOTBALL TEAM.

FR. CULLEN: We'll get the team together for you, Hank. We know where they are.

COACH: Well, where are they? [There is an embarrassed silence] What's the mystery? I ask a perfectly sane, civil, quiet and intelligent question and I get no answer. What's happened to everybody? WHERE IS THAT TEAM?

FR. CULLEN: Don't shout, Hank. — The team is — er — listening to Saint Francis of Assisi.

COACH [Looks questioningly at Father Francis]: But I thought you said—?

FR. BROOKE: This is *Father* Francis; they are listening to *Saint* Francis.

COACH: That makes sense. I suppose *Saint Francis* is briefing them on a few last-minute plays — and IF HE ISN'T I WOULD LIKE TO.

FR. LESTER: Coach, please don't shout! We have a little problem here and we were just trying to explain. — Now, why don't you go over to the gym and let us send the team to you.

COACH: Why should I go to the gym? I haven't anything to do there. I want to get the team to the airport, NOT TO THE GYM.

FR. BROOKE: Coach, Please! It was just a suggestion. You tell me where you want the team and when, and they will be there.

COACH: All right: I'd like them to eat breakfast, go to their rooms and pack, and get to the bus — IN THIRTY MINUTES — AND I'D LIKE TO WATCH!

FR. BROOKE: We'll see that they get there.

FR. LESTER: Just leave it to us.

FR. CULLEN: Brother Thomas, will you find Dutch Jones and tell him to bring the team over here right away — please.

[23]

BR. THOMAS: Just as it was getting interesting. [Goes to door] Suppose Dutch doesn't want to come?

FR. CULLEN: Just tell him.

BR. THOMAS: I understand [EXIT].

FR. BROOKE: Hank, you go get a cup of coffee and when you return we'll have the boys here.

COACH: I DON'T WANT A CUP OF COFFEE!

FR. BROOKE: THEN GET A CUP OF TEA!

COACH: O.k. [Crosses to door]: I'll be right back. [EXITS]

FR. BROOKE: Father Francis, I am sorry you had to be here while we had our little family tiff.

FR. FRANCIS [Who has been looking intently out of window at campus below, turns]: Don't apologize. — Frankly, I'm glad it happened. I've had time to think — and — it seems to me it might be better to leave the Saint with you.

FR. CULLEN: Oh, no.

FR. LESTER: You *said* you'd take him.

FR. BROOKE: You certainly did.

FR. FRANCIS: That was before I thought it through. Now I see complications — many complications.

FR. CULLEN: Just think how glorious it is for a Saint to visit you.

FR. FRANCIS: But he didn't visit me, he visited you.

FR. BROOKE: Obviously a mistake. Why should he visit the Jesuits? Our Communities are so close together — a slight slip — a slight miscalculation — and he came down on our campus instead of in your Monastery.

FR. CULLEN: You are not going to let a slight slip deprive you of the company of the Saint.

FR. LESTER: Your patron Saint — the Founder of your Order?

FR. FRANCIS: I'm not convinced it was a slip. It might be Divine Providence, and it has always been my policy not to tamper with Divine Providence. It has been a rule of my life to accept what comes.

FR. LESTER: That's what we're saying: Let Saint Francis come.

FR. FRANCIS: No, no. I think I'd better run along — will you call a taxi or do I go back in that hearse?

FR. BROOKE: You can't walk out on us. We counted on you.

FR. FRANCIS: Some other time.

FR. CULLEN: Look, if the situation were reversed, if it were Blessed Ignatius of Loyola, we'd take him off *your* hands.

[24]

FR. FRANCIS: But, you do not *realize* what a thing like this can involve: there will be investigations — embarrassment — ridicule — Catholics will frankly question our integrity and Protestants will frankly consider us a fraud — a thing like this could set Catholicism in America back a hundred years — and the Pope will have to know about it.

FR. BROOKE: We do too realize it.

FR. CULLEN [Stepping in quickly]: Father Francis, you have made the right point. You have hit the nail on the head: not just St. Ignatius University but the whole Catholic Church is involved — you have stated it so clearly. Hasn't he? — Now, if you take St. Francis home with you and keep him in the Monastery, the chance that the Church, the Faith, will be held up to ridicule will be considerably lessened.

FR. FRANCIS: I don't see why.

FR. LESTER: No one would know about him in the Monastery.

FR. BROOKE: Except the Franciscans.

FR. CULLEN: And the Franciscans won't talk!

FR. FRANCIS: Of course they'll talk — they're not the Trappists!

FR. BROOKE: Just take him back for today — your Feast Day. Then we can get organized and —

FR. CULLEN: And maybe he'll be gone.

FR. LESTER: Father Francis, there would be far less — er — *scandal* if Saint Francis were known to be preaching to the Franciscans; you see, he is talking particularly against *study and learning and the pursuit of knowledge*, and naturally his appearance in a *Jesuit University* is embarrassing, whereas if he appeared . . .

FR. FRANCIS: If you are going to say that the Franciscans put less emphasis on learning and study and the pursuit of knowledge than the Jesuits, you . . .

FR. LESTER: No, no, I didn't say that!

FR. FRANCIS: You were going to imply it.

FR. LESTER: I was not.

FR. FRANCIS: It's no use, Fathers. — You have my sympathy, but the more I consider the matter the more it seems like a Divine and, I may even add, *Benign* Providence that the Saint chose to come to you instead of to us. And, as I have said before: I do not tamper with Providence, benign, divine, or otherwise. — Good day, Fathers [Crosses to door].

FR. BROOKE: Father Francis, Wait!

FR. FRANCIS [Turning at door]: I'll take a taxi and send you the bill. [EXIT].

FR. CULLEN: There goes a wart on the Mystical Body.

FR. BROOKE: You would think he would have a little affection for his patron, just a little.

[25]

FR. LESTER: What are we going to do now?

FR. CULLEN: I wonder if they could use a *third* chaplain for the team?

FR. BROOKE: Forget it; you stay right here.

FR. CULLEN: Why me? The others have gotten out.

FR. LESTER: *I* was thinking of South America. I speak Spanish: *Hasta la vista!*

FR. BROOKE [pacing]:   This is the paradox to end paradoxes. We have in our midst the most Holy and Catholic of all the Holy Catholic Saints, and we can't get rid of him. And if he stays, not only the University but the entire religion will be held up to ridicule; the moment we announce we have Saint Francis of Assisi on our campus we will be accused of trickery, fraud and witchcraft by our enemies and by our friends of being fools. What are we going to do? The situation is embarrassing and impossible.

FR. LESTER: Saints are always embarrassing until they have been dead for a while.

FR. CULLEN: They set an uncomfortable pace.

FR. BROOKE: They can be ignored until they're canonized, but what do you do when they come back?

[BROTHER THOMAS enters unobserved]

FR. BROOKE: What do you do?

BR. THOMAS: What do you do with what?

FR. BROOKE: With a Saint, Brother Thomas. Have *you* any idea how we should proceed?

BR. THOMAS: It depends on what you have in mind.

FR. CULLEN: We have in mind convincing the world that the Saint is really — the Saint.

BR. THOMAS: That's easy: follow him; do what he tells you — convince the world of your belief by your example.

FR. BROOKE: A Jesuit follow a Franciscan?

FR. LESTER: What would St. Ignatius Loyola think?

FR. CULLEN: Never!

BR. THOMAS: St. Ignatius Loyola could appear to the Franciscans and even the score.

FR. BROOKE: Wouldn't we look silly running around in those brown robes?

BR. THOMAS: The Franciscans do all right.

FR. CULLEN: Brother Thomas, if you want to join another Order, go ahead.

FR. LESTER: Yes — why don't you?

BR. THOMAS: I have more fun with the Jesuits. — If you're interested, I couldn't find the football team.

FR. BROOKE: Couldn't find them?!

BR. THOMAS: They all left some time ago.

FR. LESTER: Is Saint Francis still speaking?

BR. THOMAS: Yes. He is elaborating on the text: "Go sell all thou hast and give to the poor." The boys seemed impressed.

FR. CULLEN: I knew I was right; I knew we should have Father Jim Sullivan here.

FR. LESTER: It certainly will interest the Vice President in Charge of Business Administration if the boys sell all they've got before they pay tuition.

FR. BROOKE: Did you get the word around that we want the football team here, right away?

BR. THOMAS: Yes, I did. I told all the boys who would listen to me — there weren't many, but I did tell them.

FR. BROOKE: Good.

BR. THOMAS: I also told the Saint you wanted to see him.

FR. LESTER: You did? Why?

BR. THOMAS: Well — I caught some of the things he is saying to the boys, and I *anticipated* that you would send for him.

FR. CULLEN: What else has he been saying?

BR. THOMAS: Oh, he's just been preaching from the Gospels — nothing very serious — if they don't take it *literally*.

FR. BROOKE: Brother Thomas, don't make a mystery out of this — what is Saint Francis saying?

BR. THOMAS: You'll find out soon . . .

[HANK HUDSON enters]

COACH: WHERE IS THAT TEAM? I DON'T SEE THEM.

FR. CULLEN: They are on the way, Hank. That's what Brother Thomas — implied — didn't you, Brother Thomas?

BR. THOMAS: Roughly.

[SAINT FRANCIS enters]

ST. FRANCIS: Did you send for me, Fathers?

FR. LESTER: Saint Francis, forgive me, but what have you been saying to the students?

COACH: *Saint Francis?!!!*

FR. BROOKE: Oh — excuse me — Friar Francis, may I introduce Hank Hudson, our coach for football; Hank — Saint Francis of Assisi.

[27]

ST. FRANCIS: "Friar" Francis.

[St. Francis inclines his head graciously; the Coach doesn't say anything —
he stares at the Saint and his head falls a little to one side, as though the
weight of the knowledge made it heavy. Father Lester leads the Coach to a
chair, and Father Cullen steps between them and the Saint.]

FR. BROOKE: We only want to know what you've told the students.

ST. FRANCIS: I talked to them of Holy Poverty and the Scriptures, and
when Brother Dutch and a goodly number of his friends rose to go, excus-
ing themselves by saying they must make a journey, I said to them: then
take nothing for your journey, neither staves nor scrip, neither shoes nor
money."

FR. BROOKE: Oh, no.

ST. FRANCIS: They assured me sweetly that they would not.

FR. CULLEN: But if they do that — it could cause —

FR. BROOKE: It certainly could.

[FATHER LESTER is shaking Hank Hudson gently by the shoulders, but
the COACH is dazed].

[DUTCH enters joyously and enthusiastically. He has obtained, somewhere,
somehow, a long, brown, tunic-looking garment tied at the waist with what
might have been an old clothes line. His appearance is not Franciscan, having neither fullness, nor sleeves, nor cowl — it is just odd and chilly looking.
He is still barefooted].

DUTCH: Did you want the team *here*, Father?

FR. BROOKE: Dutch Jones!

FR. CULLEN: Gorborduc!

FR. LESTER: Go put your clothes on!

ST. FRANCIS [Crosses to him]: Ah, Big Little Brother Dutch!

DUTCH [Pleased]: How will this do, Brother?

ST. FRANCIS: Let us go to Lady Poverty.

DUTCH: Gladly, Little Brother, but first we got to beat Iona City.

ST. FRANCIS: Iona City?

DUTCH: Yeah. They're not much of a team but they fuss a lot.

[The Coach has risen and is staring unbelievingly at Dutch]

DUTCH: We've got a much better team, Brother Francis. [Crosses to door].
I want you to see them. — Come on in boys.

[The TEAM enters, singing the school song — as many as can crowd the
stage. All are dressed similar to Dutch — all in brown, with tunics to the
ankles, some kind of rope around the waist, barefooted. They are in fine
spirits and toss a football back and forth among them.]

[28]

[HANK HUDSON passes out cold; is caught by a couple of the boys before he reaches the floor and carried out by them as they exit.]

[Before the stage is cleared, while St. Francis, hands folded contentedly, is staring at them with loving satisfaction and the Jesuit Fathers with baffled consternation—

CURTAIN

ACT TWO

SCENE 1 — THE RADIO — Saturday, October 5th, about 4 P.M.

JOE BOLAND: And Iona City takes time out! This is the fourth quarter, the last two minutes of the game between St. Ignatius and Iona City, and what a game! Iona City has failed to score all afternoon and St. Ignatius has made ten touchdowns — it's 60 *to Nothing*. This has been a fantastic football game. And here's Red Nelson with his comments about it.

RED NELSON: This is the Jesuit Football Network and the first game to be televised on the new Trans-World Television System — the whole world is watching this game. As you who have television can see: the St. Ignatius boys have no shoes and no uniforms. Yet they have played a pathetically brilliant game; they took the lead in the first quarter, just as soon as they tucked those long skirts into their girdles and stopped tripping on them, and nothing has stopped them. Shoes and money and uniforms are pouring into radio and T.V. stations all over the world — this is the first game to be televised around the world, and, believe me, the world is seeing something new in football. The President of Southern Methodist flew up during the half with uniforms from his own team, but St. Ignatius declined them.— Back to the game — here's Joe Boland.

JOE BOLAND: Play is about ready to resume — no — wait — the Iona City Captain is still protesting; it is not clear *what* he is protesting, but he *is protesting*.

Here we go at last. It's Iona's ball on their own 10 yard line; they are in punt formation — wait — there's a flag on the play. I think Iona City is being penalized for delaying the game — No! — the penalty is against St. Ignatius . . . . and it's for unsportsmanlike conduct — it's the St. Ignatius' end — His brown robe is flapping in his opponent's face.

Iona City's ball now on their own 25 yard line, first down and 10 to go. It's a long forward pass — and it's intercepted by St. Ignatius! Ralph Bilowski leaped up and picked that ball out of the air! He's running to his right — he's to the 25 — the 20 — the 15 — he's tackled — no — he's clear! He just wasn't there when the man grabbed him — He's OVER! And the score is 66 *to Nothing* in favor of St. Ignatius!

Listen to that crowd yell! Dutch Jones will hold the ball and O'Donohue is going to kick. Dutch is *back in the game* these last few minutes — he was injured in the second quarter — somebody stepped on his toe. — Here's the kick! And it's — *No Good!* And the score is still 66 *to Nothing* in favor of St. Ignatius. Now, here's Red.

[The St. Ignatius band is heard playing the school song in the background.]

RED NELSON: May we remind you again that this is the first Trans-World Television Program — the whole world is watching this game. And here are some special bulletins from the Associated Press: Britain has organized a "Bundles for America" campaign; the Soviet Ambassador has denounced St. Ignatius for sabotaging world understanding. The President of Israeli is going to pay interest on the American loan. The United Nations wants to know the true financial status of the United States and Dean Clarence Manion is going to tell them.

Now the teams are lining up — St. Ignatius will have time just to kick off and that's about all. Their kicks have been wobbly all afternoon .The boys have won this game running and *jumping*. Our experts tell us that the St. Ignatius athletes are travelling 15 to 20 pounds lighter than Iona City and it certainly has paid dividends. Once St. Ignatius takes off with the ball nobody can catch them and their high leaps on interceptions have been spectacular. — Here's the play, and here's Joe.

JOE BOLAND: Thank you, Red. We've just got seconds to go — here's the kick — and it's *short* — and there's the gun — the game is over! And the score is: *St. Ignatius* 66 - *Iona City Nothing*. — And once more, with a final word, here's Red Nelson.

RED NELSON: Just a moment. — We are going to try to take you down to the field to get a few words with the Coaches and University officials. The President and a Vice-President of St. Ignatius were here at the beginning of the game but seem to have left. — We are very sorry but apparently we cannot bring you any direct news. Hank Hudson, Coach of St. Ignatius, is just standing there with tears running down his cheeks and can't talk. We've found out that the Iona City Coach left before the game was over to confer with the National Collegiate Athletic Association and no statement was forthcoming from him . . . that could be quoted.

We will return to the air later, with more news. This is Red Nelson, your Jesuit Football Network sports announcer, wishing you "good afternoon."

ACT TWO

Scene 2

[It is Monday, October 7th — about 10 A.M.]

[When the curtain rises we are still in the President's Outer Office — even if it does look like a shoe store and mail order house. Loose shoes and shoe boxes and boxes of clothes and football uniforms line the walls and are piled in some places to the ceiling. Stacks of letters and wires are all around, and they cover the large desk to the right.]

[At the small desk, left center, is seated the Coach. He has his head on his arms, his arms on the desk, and he crying quietly to himself.]

[DUTCH JONES enters u.c. He is still wearing his long brown tunic and one big toe is bandaged. He sees the Coach and goes over and puts his hand on his shoulder.]

[30]

DUTCH: Please, Coach, we're sorry.

COACH [Without raising his head]: Go away.

DUTCH: Now, Coach, look at it like this: We didn't need the extra points, and you can't kick barefooted.

COACH [Raising his head and staring straight before him]: It couldn't happen to me. I've never done anything. I've been a good Catholic — gone to Church on Sunday, sometimes on Friday — I eat fish; I don't complain — I've never done anything.

DUTCH: Aw, Coach, don't take on about it.

COACH: I was going to quit football — retire — get a home in the country — raise pigs [Shakes head] No, not pigs — grow corn — live respectably. Then this happens. What am I going to do now?

[MAILMAN enters with a stack of mail]

MAILMAN [Bright and cheerful]: Good morning. I've got 15 registered letters and 25 with postage due. [Sees Dutch]: Say! You're one of the Barefoot Brownies! That was some game — Broth—ther!

DUTCH: Thanks. — You want me to take the mail?

MAILMAN: Can you sign for them?

DUTCH: No, but Father Brooke can. [EXIT to inner office, right, with registration slips and letters.]

MAILMAN [To Coach]: Aren't you the Football Coach here?

COACH: No. I never heard of football.

MAILMAN: We wasn't much fans either till we got a TV Saturday, and that was the first thing we seen: that football game. Do I like TV! Broth—ther!

COACH: I can't stand it.

MAILMAN: That boy there, that took the mail — was he ter-ri-fic! He caught the ball right off, but this long skirt gets in the way, and he tries to hold it up and run [grabs shoe box and tucks it under arm like a ball], but some player comes at him and he drops his skirt to push him off and then he trips on the skirt and . . .

COACH: STOP! I CAN'T STAND IT.

MAILMAN [Putting shoe box back slowly]: Say; you *really* don't like football.

COACH: No. I don't like it.

DUTCH [returning]: Here you are. [Gives him registered mail slips and money] And 85 cents.

MAILMAN: Thanks [Starts to leave and then turns back to Dutch; leads him down left, confidentially] Look, I — well, I saw the game Saturday. We got a TV — and — well — about the shoes and [pulls out two dollars].

DUTCH: Don't worry; we're O.K.

[31]

MAILMAN: It isn't much on account of we just got a TV . . .

[DUTCH and MAILMAN talk quietly down left]

[Now there staggers in u. c. a PARCEL POST MAN with boxes of shoes much higher than his head; he has to turn his back and swivel his head around to carry on a conversation. At this moment FATHER BROOKE enters from the inner office and he addresses him]

PP MAN: I brought you some more shoes.

FR. BROOKE [At desk, right, beginning to look thru mail]: Take them down to the storeroom in the basement.

PP MAN: I did. There's no space. They sent me up here.

FR. BROOKE: Try the Athletic Offices.

PP MAN: I did. They was full up an hour ago.

FR. BROOKE: All the offices?

PP MAN: Yup. — Nobody never saw so many shoes before. There must be a million pair.

FR. BROOKE: Well, set those down here. [He does and tries to arrange them in stacks] But don't bring up any more.

DUTCH [Walking the Mailman to the door]: Thanks just the same, but you understand; we *want* to go barefoot.

MAILMAN [at door]: It isn't too cold?

DUTCH: No. — Try it sometime.

MAILMAN: O.K. I will. — Yeah — I will. — Goodbye. [EXIT]

DUTCH [Cross to above desk right and begin to sort out mail]: He seems like a nice fellow.

PP MAN [Straightening up slowly]: The Postmaster quit this morning a-bout 8:00 o'clock, and the Assistant Postmaster quit at 9. They was hand-ing in resignations round there left and right. Guess by the time I get back I'll be in charge.

FR. BROOKE: Let me be the first to congratulate you. [Holds out hand]

PP MAN [Refusing it and crossing to door]: Nope. — Cause then I'd quit too.

[FATHER CULLEN enters as the PP MAN is leaving]

PP MAN: Excuse me [EXIT].

FR. CULLEN: Good morning. — Have you heard anything from the Presi-dent yet? Hello, Coach — Dutch. — Or from Father Jim Sullivan?

COACH: Hello.

DUTCH: Good morning, Father.

FR. BROOKE: They've vanished from the earth.

[32]

FR. CULLEN: I wish they hadn't taken the car with them.

FR. BROOKE: No one saw them leave the stadium.

FR. CULLEN: Do you think we ought to report it?

FR. BROOKE: No! I'm trying to keep anyone from finding out that a Saint has dropped down from Heaven — let's not suggest that the President has been taken up.

FR. CULLEN: I see your point. — Where is the Saint?

FR. BROOKE: Giving a Retreat for the team. It keeps him out of sight and the boys like him.

FR. CULLEN: He likes them too — especially since the game Saturday. He says they have a joyous spirit — he calls them Minstrels of Our Lady. Well, Coach, do you feel better this morning? [Puts hands on the coach's shoulder]

COACH: I want to resign.

FR. CULLEN: You can't resign now.

FR. BROOKE: The time isn't right.

COACH: If the time gets any righter I don't want to be here.

FR. CULLEN: You can't walk out on us now.

FR. BROOKE: What will the Iona City Coach think?

COACH: The Iona City Coach met with the National Collegiate Athletic Association Saturday night and got them to pass a new ruling.

DUTCH: I didn't hear about that.

COACH: No player can come on the field now without shoes and a *standard eighteen-pound football uniform*. They're going to *weigh the teams in*.

FR. CULLEN: But, Coach, every time St. Ignatius has a brilliant season the NCAA rewrites the rules. You're used to that.

COACH: Yeah. — BUT THIS TIME THEY MADE IT RETROACTIVE.

FR. BROOKE: You don't mean we lost the game?

COACH: I certainly do.

DUTCH: You mean Iona City won?

COACH: Yeah, Iona City won. — Iona City won: *Nothing to* 66! [Direct to Dutch]: And if we'd of made those extra points it would have been NOTHING TO 77! — I resign. [Crosses to door].

FR. BROOKE: Coach — Wait!

FR. CULLEN: Don't go!

DUTCH: Aw, Coach!

COACH [at door]: You may forward my check. Goodbye. [Exit]

[33]

FR. BROOKE: Now we've got to get someone to take over his job.

FR. CULLEN: What about the Freshman coach? He's young and . . .

DUTCH: He didn't come back with the team, Father.

FR. BROOKE: Don't tell me he's disappeared!

DUTCH: I don't know whether he's disappeared, but he isn't around. Nobody is.

FR. BROOKE [to Father Cullen]:   Appointing a new coach is the President's job — and Father Eddy's bound to come back sooner or later. So is Father Jim.

FR. CULLEN: I don't know. I wouldn't if I were he.

DUTCH [Still sorting and opening the mail]:   Here's a card for you, Father Brooke. It's marked "Personal."

FR. BROOKE [Taking it]:   It's the President's handwriting.

FR. CULLEN: What does it say?

FR. BROOKE [reading]:   "Making a Retreat — may remain — Eddy and Jim."

FR. CULLEN: Where are they?

FR. BROOKE [turning the card over and looking at the picture]:   It says: "Our Lady of Gethsemani Monastery, Trappist, Kentucky. [He hands it to Father Cullen, who studies it].

FR. CULLEN: It's a good idea.

[FATHER LESTER enters; he is in good spirits]

FR. LESTER: Ah, still getting mail.

FR. CULLEN: Yes.

FR. BROOKE: We have some new problems.

[Father Cullen hands Father Lester the President's card.]

FR. LESTER: I was just getting used to the old ones. [reads card] This is very simple: Father Phil, you take over.

FR. BROOKE: I will not. — I thought we could draw straws.

FR. LESTER [looking at Father Cullen]:   I think it's unanimous among the Vice Presidents present, except you, of course, that you are elected . . .

FR. CULLEN: Entirely unanimous.

FR. LESTER: Until such time as the new President is appointed by the Provincial.

FR. LESTER: What are you doing with all the mail? [Begins to run thru some of it]

[34]

FR. BROOKE: We are taking out the checks and loose money and we are going to answer all of them — as soon as we can figure out a form letter that won't sound too silly.

FR. LESTER [His attention is caught by one of the envelopes]: Oh — Oh — [Opens it]: "Propagation of the Faith."

FR. CULLEN: What is it?

FR. LESTER [holding up $10 bill]: "Here's $10 I was saving for a new breviary — buy shoes for the boys — God Love You — Fulton Sheen."

FR. CULLEN: We've heard from everybody now but the Pope.

FR. BROOKE: That will come.

[BROTHER THOMAS enters]

BR. THOMAS: Father Brooke, the Saint wants to see you.

FR. BROOKE: Where is he?

BR. THOMAS: Just outside.

FR. BROOKE: But I thought we had fixed it for him to spend the day in retreat.

BR. THOMAS: I wouldn't know about that. He just said he wanted to ask you a question.

FR. BROOKE [looks helplessly at others]: All right, Bring him in.

FR. LESTER: Dutch, you'd better go in the other room.

DUTCH: Yes, Father.

FR. LESTER: And take some mail with you.

DUTCH: O.K., Father. [Exit to inner office, right].

FR. CULLEN: Does anybody know the Saint is on the campus?

FR. BROOKE: There's a kind of "feeling" that he is someone special, but since he always introduces himself as Friar Francis they think he is just an odd Franciscan — I believe. I'm not sure.

[SAINT FRANCIS enters, meekly]

FR. BROOKE: Ah, Brother Francis, good morning, we are very happy to have you here.

[Father Lester looks at Father Brooke sharply]

ST. FRANCIS: Good morning, Fathers.

FR. LESTER and FR. CULLEN: Good morning.

FR. BROOKE: You wanted to see me?

ST. FRANCIS: Yes.

FR. BROOKE: Anything wrong with the boys?

[35]

ST. FRANCIS: Oh, no, Father. I love the Big Little Brothers. What disturbs me is *education in Kansas*. I cannot understand it.

FR. BROOKE: It's the same all over the United States.

ST. FRANCIS: What is that, Father?

FR. BROOKE: It is difficult to explain the United States — but is anything especially troubling you?

ST. FRANCIS: I have been talking to your PhD's—

FR. BROOKE: Yes?

ST. FRANCIS: — and to your M.A.'s —

FR. BROOKE: Yes?

ST. FRANCIS: —and I do not find that a PhD loves God any more than an M.A.

FR. CULLEN: That could be.

ST. FRANCIS: So I wish to know why you divide them into A.B.'s, M.A.'s, and PhD's.

[There is a moment's silence]

FR. BROOKE [on a real inspiration]: Father Lester here is Vice President of our entire Field of Studies — he will explain our educational theory. Father Lester.

FR. LESTER: Yes. — Well. — It is out dominating purpose through the instrumentality of intelligence and truth to assist the student in gaining control of his *tendential dynamism*. We keep in personal contact with the *preconscious spiritual dynamism* of human personality and through both the irrational subconscious and the preconscious of the spirit evolve a deep *internal dynamism*. We help the student overcome the inner multiplicity of the diverse vital energies at play in his mind, and through the very intuitivity traversing our teaching we expand his interiority to himself. In short, Frater, we educate *the whole man*.

FR. CULLEN: That's the first time I've understood it. — We ought to raise the tuition again.

ST. FRANCIS: I still don't understand: If a PhD doesn't love God more than an A.B., why do they go to school?

[BROTHER THOMAS enters, u. c.]

BR. THOMAS: There is a reporter out here and he sure is good and mad.

FR. BROOKE: What is he mad about?

BR. THOMAS: He says there is a saint on this campus and he is going to find him.

FR. CULLEN: Friar Francis, would you please wait for us a moment in the President's Office?

[36]

ST. FRANCIS: I would like to return to the team.

FR. LESTER: I'll take you back myself in just a few minutes. — Please, Friar Francis. [Leads him to door of inner office.]

ST. FRANCIS: I hope it will not be long. I have much to say to them [Exit].

FR. BROOKE: O.K. Send the reporter in, Brother Thomas.

BR. THOMAS: Can I watch?

FR. BROOKE: No. [Brother Thomas exits, u. c.]

FR. CULLEN: How have you kept the reporters off this long?

FR. LESTER: And the telephone? Why doesn't that ring?

FR. BROOKE: Somebody cut the wire.

FR. CULLEN: Now who would have done that?

FR. BROOKE: Me. — If you had been here at 8 o'clock this morning you would have cut the wire too. Incidentally, where were you both?

[MILTON HOFFMAN enters briskly, u. c, with his camera. His face and hands are scratched and he has a few tears in his clothes.]

HOFFMAN: Good morning, Fathers. I am Milt Hoffman, representing STRIFE magazine and, right now, 500 other reporters. What's the idea of putting barbed wire around the campus?

FR. BROOKE: Well — uh — after the game Saturday we were beseiged with so many publicity hounds it got embarrassing. We didn't realize the press wanted to reach us.

HOFFMAN: I want to see the President.

FR. CULLEN: He's *not in*.

HOFFMAN: Where is he?

FR. LESTER: He's *out*.

HOFFMAN: What is he doing?

FR. BROOKE [glancing at his wrist watch]: Praying, I imagine.

HOFFMAN: I hope he'll pray for me — because I'm about to break the Fifth Commandment — I'm going to murder somebody.

FR. BROOKE: Then we'll pray for you, too. — This is Father Cullen — Father Lester — and I am Father Brooke.

HOFFMAN: Pleased to meet you. — And now can you tell me: where is Murphy? Where is *anybody* in Public Relations?

FR. BROOKE: There's no one down there?

HOFFMAN: No one. — And believe me: St. Ignatius is going to need some public relations. — Do you know what people are saying about this place?

[37]

FR. CULLEN: They're talking about us?

HOFFMAN: "Talking about!!!" — They say you have a *Saint* on the campus!

FR. CULLEN and FATHER LESTER: A Saint!

DUTCH [entering from inner office]: Fathers, excuse me, I . . .

FR. LESTER: Come *right on through,* Dutch. — Close the door. — You won't disturb us.

DUTCH [Closes door obediently]: But I only want to tell you that the . . .

FR. LESTER: Certainly, Dutch. Go right on out. *Don't say another word* Just go along. [Leads Dutch to door, u. c.]

DUTCH: It's only that the . . .

FR. BROOKE: Dutch! When you start to leave a room, leave. Don't dawdle. Go!

DUTCH [bewildered now]: Yes, Father. [Exit, u. c.]

FR. BROOKE: We try to teach our students manners.

FR. CULLEN: We try to educate *the whole man.*

FR. BROOKE: Now, Mr. Hoffman, you were saying?

HOFFMAN: I said: "they said you had a Saint on the campus."

FR. CULLEN: Who is "they?"

HOFFMAN [Loudly]: Everybody! [More quietly] Does it make any difference who? Is there a Saint on the campus, or isn't there?

FR. BROOKE: Mr. Hoffman, sit down and let us explain something to you. Please. [Hoffman is reluctant, but Father Lester pulls a chair down left and Hoffman sits, facing front; Father Brooke is on his left and Frs. Lester and Cullen on his right, blocking the sight of the office door from both Hoffman and Father Brooke.]

FR. LESTER: Mr. Hoffman, you are not a Catholic, are you?

HOFFMAN: No, and what's that got to do with it?

[At this moment, St. Francis opens the door right, walks quietly and unobserved through the room and out the door up center.]

FR. BROOKE: It is just that among Catholics the word *Saint* has many meanings. We sometimes call the Angels and Archangels saints — you've heard the phrase "Saint Michael, the Archangel," haven't you?

HOFFMAN: No.

FR. BROOKE: Well, we use it. We use it for Angels, and for Saints in Heaven, and also for members of the Church on earth; that is, we call ourselves "saints" in the sense that we are destined to be saints. Now therefore . .

HOFFMAN: Look, Father, I don't want to take instructions: I just want

[38]

to know is there a Saint on the Campus — a real one — not you or the Fathers here, but a real bonified one walking around?

FR. BROOKE [gently and a little piously]: But that is what I have been trying to explain: There are many saints on the Campus, in the broad Catholic sense.

HOFFMAN: I'm interested in just one.

FR. CULLEN: Which one?

HOFFMAN: St. Ignatius Loyola! Has St. Ignatius Loyola appeared on this campus or hasn't he?

FR. CULLEN and FR. LESTER: He hasn't.

FR. BROOKE: He certainly hasn't.

FR. LESTER: Except in spirit. He is always present in spirit.

HOFFMAN: I am not talking about his spirit. I get reports that he's out preaching on the campus, but nobody tells me anything straight. I've tried to contact your publicity office, I've talked to the students, I've . . .

FR. BROOKE: What do the students say?

HOFFMAN: A lot of double-talk just the way you do. — [Rises and walks left] I'm sorry, Fathers, but I've got to write a story — take pictures and [at this point he is pacing by the windows and looking down sees something on campus] — excuse me. [Starts rapidly for door] I'll be back [Exit, u.c.]

FR. BROOKE: Wait a minute! [But Hoffman has gone] What did he see?

[Crosses to windows, where he is joined by Frs. Lester and Cullen.]

FR. CULLEN: It's Saint Francis!

FR. LESTER: It can't be — he's in the office.

FR. BROOKE: It's *bi-location.*

[They all tear over to the door, right; Fr. Lester throws it open and looks in].

FR. LESTER: It's *not* bi-location — he isn't here — just there!

FR. BROOKE: Are you sure?

FR. LESTER: Look for yourself.

[They do, and then all start back to the windows]

FR. CULLEN: But how do you account for his being out there?

FR. LESTER: I don't account for it.

FR. BROOKE: I wonder what he is going to do now.

FR. LESTER: Looks like he's getting ready to preach.

FR. CULLEN: I wish he wouldn't climb on the statue of St. Ignatius.

FR. LESTER: He is so small he has to — to be seen. [Turns away from window].

[39]

FR. BROOKE: Oh no — no — no!

FR. LESTER [turning back]: What is it?

FR. CULLEN: As soon as the students saw him barefooted they took off their shoes!

FR. LESTER: They'll all catch cold.

FR. BROOKE: I hope the staff at the Infirmary doesn't make a retreat.

FR. CULLEN: There's the photographer.

FR. BROOKE: He's taking out his camera. [Walks center].

FR. LESTER [Also leaving window]: *I'd* like to take the next train to the Trappist Monastery.

FR. BROOKE: You'll stay right here. We're all in this together.

FR. CULLEN [Leaving window too]: Frankly, I don't see why.

FR. LESTER: Neither do I.

FR. BROOKE: Well, for one thing, you just voted me in charge and *Holy Obedience* is telling you to *stay.*

[PROFESSOR EINSTEIDER rushes in — stops and looks around. Professor Einsteider has a thick German accent]

FR. BROOKE [amiably]: Ah, Professor Einsteider, what can we do for you?

EINSTEIDER: Where are my students?

FR. BROOKE: What do you mean?

EINSTEIDER: Not one student for Mathematics this morning — I waited for *them* 20 *minutes!* Where are they?

FR. LESTER: Didn't you come across the campus?

EINSTEIDER: No. I cut through the back gate.

FR. CULLEN: Look out of the window.

[All watch as Einsteider crosses to window and looks out]

EINSTEIDER: Who is that preaching?

FR. BROOKE: Saint Francis of Assisi.

EINSTEIDER: St. Francis of Assisi! I thought he was dead!

FR. CULLEN: Anybody can be mistaken.

[BROTHER THOMAS enters. Professor Einsteider continues to stare out of the window.]

BR. THOMAS: Father Brooke, there is a man here from Washington who wants to see the President. I told him he'd left town so he wants to see you.

FR. BROOKE: Who is he?

[40]

BR. THOMAS: He says he's Secretary to the Secretary of State.

FR. BROOKE: Ask him in.

FR. CULLEN: This ought to be good.

FR. LESTER: I wonder how he got through the barbed wire.

EINSTEIDER [without turning around]: No shoes.

FR. LESTER: I hope the Saint on our Campus hasn't affected Washington.

EINSTEIDER: They're taking off their coats.

[BROTHER THOMAS shows in JOHN OWEN STEWART, a Washington diplomat of the silk handerchief school; he carries a portfolio.]

BR. THOMAS: This is Mr. John Owen Stewart, Secretary to Secretary Dulles, — Father Brooke — Father Lester — Father Cullen.

STEWART: Good morning.

FATHERS ALL: Good morning.

[Brother Thomas leaves.]

FR. BROOKE: Won't you sit down?

[STEWART looks around at the boxes, shoes and general disarray with distaste—he looks as though he would like to flip the dust off the chair with his silk handkerchief before he sat down.]

FR. BROOKE [seeing him glance about]: Oh — excuse the condition of the office. Just a few — er — [waves a hand helplessly in the direction of the mess.]

STEWART: I will be very brief, gentlemen.

FR. BROOKE: Thank you.

STEWART: This situation that you have — *created* — has caused . . .

FR. BROOKE: We didn't *create* it.

STEWART: You *fostered* it.

FR. CULLEN: I don't know that I would say that.

FR. LESTER: Could we say that we *permitted* it?

FR. BROOKE: That is more accurate

FR. CULLEN: Much more.

STEWART: Gentlemen, may I continue?

FR. BROOKE: Of course.

STEWART: This situation, however it arose, is disturbing to the President of the United States.

FR. LESTER: No!

[41]

STEWART: Yesterday he snapped at Mamie and today his golf score went up.

FR. CULLEN: That's bad.

STEWART: That football game was televised around the world and now governments the world over are cabling money to Washington. — You know how *hard* President Eisenhower has worked to *raise* the *debt limit?*

FR. LESTER: Everybody knows that.

STEWART: Well, if this continues: in another 24 hours the Government of the United States will become *solvent.*

FR. BROOKE [Makes clicking sound of sympathy].

STEWART: Do you realize that there is *no one* in Washington, Republican or Democrat, who knows how to run a solvent economy. [Proudly] We *think* in the *red.*

FR. LESTER: But couldn't something be done to put us back in debt?

STEWART: Gentlemen — before that football game Saturday our national debt was two hundred and eighty billion dollars, and it took us over 22 years to build it — you can't expect us to do it again overnight.

FR. BROOKE: No, no. I guess not.

STEWART: Gentlemen, President Eisenhower has *made* a *decision.* [He opens his portfolio here and consults papers during his next speeches] Realizing that the world crisis has arisen as a result of *mismanagement* at St. Ignatius, he has created an agency to help you *reorganize* your internal affairs. He calls it the National Welfare Fund for Football for St. Ignatius. The NWFFFFSTI — and it will operate under the TVA.

FR. LESTER: But why put St. Ignatius under the Tennessee Valley Authority?

STEWART: *Because,* if we *tuck* you in there, it will take *years* for an investigating committee to *find* you.

FR. CULLEN: That's good.

STEWART: The National Director was appointed this morning, with national offices in Washington, naturally, and a branch office will be set up here the end of the week. — Now, about office space —

FR. BROOKE: Why do you want office space?

STEWART: The NWFFFFSTI will run the University, of course, and will require a staff of, let's see [runs through papers] — we figure about two hundred and fifty . . .

FR. BROOKE: Two hundred and fifty!

STEWART: Two hundred and fifty executives — five hundred secretaries — and a publicity staff of one hundred and fifty — making a total of nine hundred. — Don't worry about housing — Federal Housing will take care of that.

[42]

FR. BROOKE: Do the two hundred and fifty executives know they will have to become *Jesuits?*

STEWART [putting the papers back]: The NWFFFFSTI will, naturally, take care of *any dues.*

FR. BROOKE: There is also an initiation — takes about fourteen years, and everybody isn't chosen.

[Stewart looks around to see if they are serious about this.]

FR. CULLEN: That's right. Maybe longer with executives.

STEWART [rising and snapping his portfolio]: I shall tell Mr. Dulles to tell President Eisenhower's secretary to tell President Eisenhower what you have said.

FR. BROOKE: Good! and we'll tell Clare Booth Luce to tell the Pope.

STEWART: Good day, gentlemen. [He bows and exits]

EINSTEIDER: No, no, no, no, no. [Turns from window] I cannot stand Americans. I will go back to Germany. [Paces right] Americans—bah!

[The others have heard this before and say nothing]

EINSTEIDER: I will resign from this University. I cannot live in America. I cannot breathe the air. Than teach American students I would rather be a plumber.

BR. THOMAS [appearing in the doorway just in time to catch this remark]: If you have any talent for it, Professor Einsteider, there's a leaky faucet in the basement.

EINSTEIDER: *Dummkopf!* [Exit]

FR. BROOKE: What is the trouble now, Brother?

BR. THOMAS: Mike Dunnovan, National President of the St. Ignatius Alumni Association, is downstairs.

FR. LESTER: I've been expecting this.

BR. THOMAS: He seems pretty upset.

FR. CULLEN: Did the guard let him in the gate, or did he come through the barbed wire?

BR. THOMAS: The guard let him in.

FR. BROOKE: Good! He's been mad ever since we hired Professor Einsteider and I don't want him to get any madder. — Ask him up.

[MILT HOFFMAN tears through the door waving a negative — Brother Thomas slips out behind him]

HOFFMAN: He didn't take! — He didn't take!

FR. CULLEN: What's the matter?

FR. LESTER: Who didn't take what?

HOFFMAN: That preacher out there — I took him and he didn't take! — I took his picture and he's not in it.

FR. BROOKE: Let me see. [takes print] No, he isn't. Look! [Hands it to Father Cullen, who hands it on to Father Lester]

FR. CULLEN: Strange.

FR. LESTER: Very strange.

HOFFMAN: *Who — is — he?*

FR. BROOKE: He is a Catholic Saint, and I tried to explain to you before about Catholic Saints, but you wouldn't listen.

HOFFMAN: All I want to know is: which one is he? What does he do?

FR. BROOKE: Father Cullen, why don't you tell Mr. Hoffman *all about* St. Francis?

FR. CULLEN [Understanding]: All right, Father. [To Hoffman]: Pull up a chair, Mr. Hoffman, and take notes.

[Hoffman sits at desk right — Father Cullen clears space for him and they begin to converse]

FR. CULLEN: Blessed Saint Francis was born in Assisi in 1182 . . .

HOFFMAN: "Assisi" . . . When?

[FATHER CULLEN stands between Hoffman and the audience and continues giving facts; meanwhile MICHAEL DUNNOVAN has entered. A handsome, middle-aged businessman, usually well groomed, he looks as though he hasn't been to bed for two nights, which is the case].

FR. BROOKE: Ah, come in, Mike. We're glad to see you. [Holds out hand].

DUNNOVAN [Clasping his hand — hardly able to speak]: Father — why didn't you tell us? — Father Lester.

FR. LESTER: Glad to see you, Mike.

DUNNOVAN: The Alumni Association — we knew you were having difficulties — but — we had no idea you had reached such straits!

FR. BROOKE: We didn't *want* you to know.

DUNNOVAN: But it was the *right* of the Alumni to know — the disgrace — poor Father Eddy — Poor Father Eddy! — How did he take it?

FR. LESTER: The best way possible.

HOFFMAN [as Father Cullen moves back, clearing him for the audience a moment]: "Founded the Franciscan Order" [He is writing] When?

FR. CULLEN: Twelve hundred and ten.

DUNNOVAN [overlapping end of Father Cullen's speech]: I don't want you to feel that the Alumni Association has let the University down, because we haven't. I have flown from New York to Los Angeles and back since Saturday and we have started a drive that will make you the richest

[44]

university in the country — in the world! We are going to see to it that St. Ignatius has everything every other University has got — three times over — *four* times!

FR. LESTER: We wouldn't want you to go to that much trouble.

FR. CULLEN: Canonized in 1228 and . . .

DUNNOVAN: We're hitting every alumnus in this country, and abroad. We've even hit a couple of Cardinals. We're going to get you an endowment *four times as big as Harvard's — four times as —* Say! What is Harvard's?

FR. LESTER: I believe it is 265 million.

FR. BROOKE: But a billion would do.

FR. LESTER: Yes, we would be very happy with a billion dollar university.

DUNNOVAN: *A billion dollars!*

[Enter WESTERN UNION MESSENGER with cable]

WESTERN UNION: I have a cable for you — anybody take it?

FR. CULLEN: I'll sign for it.

FR. BROOKE: Where is it from?

FR. CULLEN: The Vatican!

FR. LESTER: What did you say?

FR. CULLEN [Handing the slip to Western Union]: Thanks. [Western Union exits] The Vatican!

FR. BROOKE: The Vatican! Open it!

FR. CULLEN: It's half English, half Italian.

FR. LESTER: Give it here.

[While Father Lester reads the long cable, Dunnovan looks baffled and keeps muttering: "a billion dollar drive — a billion dollar drive"; and Hoffman, with notes in one hand and negative in the other, repeats: "Born 1182 — Franciscan Order 1210 — doesn't take picture."]

FR. CULLEN: What does it say?

FR. LESTER: It's pretty technical — and sort of garbled.

FR. BROOKE: Just give us the gist of it.

FR. LESTER: The gist of it is: *Answer the phone or be excommunicated!*

CURTAIN

[45]

ACT III

[The scene is the same. The shoe boxes and clothing have been cleared away and the office restored to normal.

[It is Thursday, October 10th — about 3 P.M.

[Father Francis, the Franciscan, is pacing up and down. He has a STRIFE magazine rolled up in his hand.

[FATHER BROOKE enters from inner office]

FR. BROOKE: Ah, Father Francis, what can we do for you?

FR. FRANCIS: We want our Saint.

FR. BROOKE: Now, Father Francis, you musn't be selfish. St. Francis of Assisi belongs to the world, and if he chooses to be our guest now . . .

FR. FRANCIS: He made a mistake.

FR. BROOKE: I don't think so. — Confidentially, Father Francis, we have all learned to love the Saint. He has brought something into our lives—he has become a part of us.

FR. FRANCIS: No Franciscan could ever become a part of the Jesuits.

FR. BROOKE: And he has done a great deal for the University—a great deal.

FR. FRANCIS: I've heard about that billion dollar drive.

FR. BROOKE: We are going to be solvent and *we* understand how to run a solvent economy.

FR. FRANCIS: That money isn't yours.

FR. BROOKE: What money isn't whose?

FR. FRANCIS: St. Francis of Assisi is a Franciscan and any money coming to you through him should come to us.

FR. BROOKE: Wait a minute!

FR. FRANCIS: That's what the Franciscan lawyers say.

FR. BROOKE: Wait till you hear what the Jesuit lawyers say. — If this is the purpose of your visit, you can consider your time wasted.

FR. FRANCIS: It is only half of the purpose—the other half is to take the Saint back with me.

FR. BROOKE: I repeat: you can consider the visit wasted.

FR. FRANCIS: He is *our* Saint.

FR. BROOKE: Ah, yes—but a *Divine,* and I may add, *Benign,* Providence sent him to us—and he remains.

FR. FRANCIS: I do not believe Providence intended to make fools of the Franciscans! [Father Brooke says nothing]—Have you seen this week's STRIFE?

[46]

FR. BROOKE: No.

FR. FRANCIS [holding it out]: There's a *drawing* of St. Francis on the cover . . .

FR. BROOKE [Looking at it]: The photographer never got a picture.

FR. FRANCIS: . . . and the caption is: "Switched to Jesuits."

FR. BROOKE: It's not a very good likeness. [flipping thru pages] What's the story?

FR. FRANCIS: Football.

FR. BROOKE [reading]: "Franciscan Inspires Jeusit Eleven in Victorious Defeat"—nothing about the life of the Saint. Father Cullen will be disappointed.

FR. FRANCIS: What do you intend to do?

FR. BROOKE: I am not going to do anything, because I don't have to do anything. And besides, I like the Saint; I find him . . .

[SAINT FRANCIS enters, u.c]

FR. BROOKE: Ah, Friar Francis.

FR. FRANCIS [in spite of himself, he is moved]: The Saint!

ST. FRANCIS: Good morning, Fathers.

FR. BROOKE: Friar Francis, may I introduce Father Francis—of Assisi.

ST. FRANCIS: Good morning, Father.

FR. FRANCIS: Good morning.

ST. FRANCIS: I too am from Assisi, Father.

FR. FRANCIS: Yes—I—know.

FR. BROOKE: Father Francis was just leaving—weren't you, Father? [holds out hand] Goodbye, Father.

FR. FRANCIS [refusing to shake hands]: I was not.—[crosses to St. Francis] Saint Francis, we want . . .

ST. FRANCIS: "Friar" Francis.

FR. FRANCIS: Friar Francis, we Franciscans want you to return to us.

ST. FRANCIS: I don't understand.

FR. FRANCIS: We want you to be with your own friars.

ST. FRANCIS: But I am with my own friars—my own Brothers—Brother Halfback, Brother Quarterback, Brother Fullback . . .

FR. FRANCIS: They're not Franciscans. They're the Jesuit Football Team.

ST. FRANCIS: They became Friars this morning.

FR. BROOKE: They what!!?

[47]

ST. FRANCIS: They became Friars.

FR. BROOKE: No, no — they can't!

ST. FRANCIS: I don't understand.

FR. BROOKE: You can't have a football team under Holy Obedience to a Saint. — And they play Michigan State on Saturday.

ST. FRANCIS: I liked the football game. My Big Little Brothers were like joyous minstrels—troubadors—they were gladiators for Our Lady.

FR. FRANCIS [aside]: He's been reading Chesterton.

ST. FRANCIS: I shall look forward to the game.

FR. BROOKE: There won't be a game if the boys don't wear shoes, and the standard 18 pounds . . .

[THE PHONE RINGS]

FR. BROOKE [crossing to it rapidly]: I'll get it.—Excuse me. — Hello. — Who—What?—Of course not! We're a college, not a country.—But we would look silly sending a representative to the United Nations. Goodbye.— [to the others] The United Nations wants to pool our financial resources with atomic energy.

FR. FRANCIS: Friar Francis, your appearance here has brought this university untold wealth—they can't even count the money—they're going to have a billion dollars. And they're Jesuits!

FR. BROOKE: We don't have it yet.

ST. FRANCIS: Is that a lot of money?

FR. BROOKE: Not today.

FR. FRANCIS: Well it isn't bad for a university that never knew how it would meets its next deficit.

ST. FRANCIS [gently]: *How* has my being with you brought you wealth, Father?

FR. BROOKE: Well—you see—Saturday's game was televised around the world—

ST. FRANCIS: What?

FR. BROOKE: —and when the people saw our boys barefooted, they felt sorry for them and — er —

ST. FRANCIS: Why?

FR. BROOKE: They thought they couldn't buy shoes.

ST. FRANCIS: Didn't you explain?

FR. BROOKE: We *need* the money.

ST. FRANCIS: Why?

FR. BROOKE: To run the university — to teach the students —

[43]

ST. FRANCIS: To make A.B.'s?

FR. BROOKE: Yes.

ST. FRANCIS: And M.A.'s?

FR. BROOKE: Yes.

ST. FRANCIS: And PhD's?

FR. BROOKE: Yes.

ST. FRANCIS: Father: give the money back.

FR. BROOKE: But, Friar Francis, you don't understand; we must *educate* our boys.

ST. FRANCIS: If you would educate them, teach them to put aside material things—teach them to work with their hands and to serve with their hearts, and all else will follow. [pleading] And now, I beg you, Father, *please give back the money you have received through me.*

FR. BROOKE: But we can't just . . .

ST. FRANCIS: I implore you.

FR. FRANCIS: Well, I must be going [starts to door].

FR. BROOKE: Wait! You wanted to take Saint Francis back with you.

FR. FRANCIS: He refused the invitation. Good day, Father, Good day, Friar.

FR. BROOKE [starting after him]: I want to talk to you.

FR. FRANCIS: Some other time. [exit]

[There is a moment's silence. Father Brooke faces Saint Francis and for the first time he realizes that he is in the presence of a great Saint. Before this he has been too busy thinking about St. Ignatius University to permit any personal impact. Now he knows this is an important moment for him and he cannot think of a thing to say.]

FR. BROOKE: Friar Francis — ?

ST. FRANCIS: Yes, Father Brooke?

FR. BROOKE: —Won't you sit down?

ST. FRANCIS: Thank you, Father.

[Both sit, and there is silence again.]

FR. BROOKE: Friar Francis — I want you to know that you are most welcome at St. Ignatius University.

ST FRANCIS: Thank you, Father Brooke.

FR. BROOKE: In fact, ever since you arrived, I have wanted to talk you alone. — I — er [He stops completely and there is silence again]

ST. FRANCIS: Yes, Father? — You can tell me what is troubling you.

[49]

FR. BROOKE [low and confidentially]: Friar Francis—how does it feel to go barefooted? — You see, when I was very young I wanted to be a Franciscan too—but, somehow, I don't quite know myself how, I wound up a Jesuit.

ST. FRANCIS [jumping up delightedly]: Ah, Father, I knew it! I knew it! You will come with me and my new Friars—we need you.

FR. BROOKE: Do you really want me?

ST. FRANCIS: Of course we want you—you belong to us.

FR. BROOKE: I do?

ST. FRANCIS: Yes. This is exactly what I dreampt last night.

FR. BROOKE: Then here goes. [sitting in chair behind desk right, he takes off his shoes and socks rapidly and steps out into the middle of the room] Ah . . . [he walks down left]

ST. FRANCIS: Now I am free to leave. All will be well with my little Friars.

FR. BROOKE: What do you mean?

ST. FRANCIS: You will take care of them for me—guide them for me. Goodbye, Father Brooke. [starts for door]

FR. BROOKE: No—wait! You can't do this.

ST. FRANCIS [at door]: Goodbye, *sweet* Father Brooke. [exit]

[Father Brooke starts to follow—gets to door, but draws quickly back and dashes behind desk right to try to get his shoes on. But he hasn't time because Father Cullen and Father Lester enter very quickly. Father Brooke sticks his shoes and feet under the desk.]

FR. CULLEN [waving letter]: Phil—do you know what's happened now?

FR. LESTER: This whole situation is getting ridiculous—it's out of hand.

FR. BROOKE: I can't imagine anything more ridiculous than what's already happened.

FR. CULLEN: You know that Discalced Order of Franciscans in Canada?

FR. BROOKE: I believe I've heard of them.

FR. CULLEN: They accuse us of making them look silly.

FR. BROOKE: How could Jesuits in Kansas make Franciscans in Canada look silly?

FR. LESTER: They claim our going barefooted has brought ridicule on all Orders of barefoot friars.

FR. CULLEN: They make no distinction between football players and priests.

FR. LESTER: Of course, we have only to explain that no *Jesuit* has gone barefooted.

FR. BROOKE: Of course.

[50]

FR. CULLEN: And that will certainly settle the matter.

FR. BROOKE: It certainly will.

FR. LESTER: They threaten to sue—but we know that's an idle threat, and anyhow there's no evidence whatsoever that any Jesuit has ever gone barefooted.

FR. BROOKE: No evidence whatsoever.

FR. CULLEN: You sound a little strained, Phil. Is all this confusion getting you down?

FR. BROOKE: No — no — I'm taking it in my stride — I hope [Sticks feet further under desk]

FR. LESTER: I'm worn out. Since the phones are working and the barbed wire is down, there isn't a moment's peace—day or night. [Sits down]

FR. CULLEN: I said my Divine Office at one o'clock this morning—yesterday's. [Also sits] Yesterday's!

FR. BROOKE: You are mixed up.

FR. LESTER: Oh, Phil — I know what I wanted to tell you.

FR. BROOKE: What?

FR. LESTER: The Shoemakers' Union is picketing the Campus.

FR. BROOKE: No! — What do they want?

FR. CULLEN: They want everybody to wear shoes — They are afraid this fad will spread and put them out of business.

FR. BROOKE: No.

FR. CULLEN: We're trying to assure them that it's limited to a few boys.

FR. BROOKE: Good.

FR. LESTER: You certainly look tired, Phil. Don't you want to go to your room? We'll take over for a while.

FR. BROOKE: No — no! I want to stay *right here*. I'm *going* to stay right here. Why don't you two take an hour off?

FR. LESTER: We wouldn't desert you now.

FR. CULLEN: Positively not!

FR. BROOKE: But I *insist* — I — Oh. what's the use! — Bob — Louis — I talked to Saint Francis alone — while you were out and he convinced me that [he has risen and is about to step from behind the desk when

[MIKE DUNNOVAN enters, u.c. He is even more haggard than ever, but still dynamic, still on the ball]

MIKE: Good afternoon, Fathers. I've got the check. [Pulls it out]

FR. LESTER and FR. CULLEN: Good afternoon, Mike.

[51]

FR. BROOKE [Back behind the desk]: Good afternoon.

DUNNOVAN [holding check up]: Just like I said: it's for *one billion dollars.*

[He holds it toward Father Brooke, who, after the slighest hesitation, makes a long reach over the desk for it, having to balance with one hand to make it. Father Brooke then looks at it carefully and says nothing.]

DUNNOVAN: Is there anything wrong with it?

FR. BROOKE: No.

FR. CULLEN: Let me see it. [Goes over to take it]

FR. LESTER: You don't seem very enthusiastic. [He gets it after Fr. Cullen]

FR. BROOKE: Somehow, it dosn't look the way I expected it to.

DUNNOVAN: What did you expect, Father?

FR. BROOKE: I don't know — It just looks like any other check.

DUNNOVAN: Did you want it embossed in gold?

FR. BROOKE [Snapping to and remembering the formalities]: Through me, Mike, the University thanks the National Alumni Association of St. Ignatius, through you.

DUNNOVAN: For the National Alumni Association of St. Ignatius, I accept your thanks. [Starts to door] And if there is anything *else* we can do at any time — No! — No! — What am I saying — *That's it!* Goodbye! [Exit]

FR. CULLEN: You seem disappointed, Phil. — The financial problems of St. Ignatius are over. [Crosses to windows and looks out] Whatever else happens to us, we will not have to worry again about money.

FR. LESTER: There will probably be a lot of other things to worry about though. I think I'll go back to my office. [Starts to door and stops]. Somehow, I have a premonition that something else is about to happen.

FR. BROOKE: I just wouldn't pay any attention to it.

[Enter BROTHER THOMAS]

BR. THOMAS: Father Brooke — the Saint was praying in the Chapel and then he walked up toward the Altar and disappeared.

FR. LESTER: Nonsense.

BR. THOMAS: He disappeared.

FR. LESTER: Oh, Brother Thomas, first you see saints, and then you don't. [Brother Thomas look at him hard]—[to the others]: Do you suppose he is really gone?

FR. BROOKE: That's funny.

FR. CULLEN: What's funny about it?

FR. BROOKE: If he's gone — and we're not sure *why* he came.

[52]

FR. LESTER: I never thought of that. He must have had a *purpose* in coming . . .

FR. BROOKE: I feel very strongly that he did — and I don't think it was to make us rich.

FR. LESTER: We aren't sure that he has really gone.

BR. THOMAS: I am.

FR. CULLEN [Who has been looking out the window during the last few speeches]: I am too.

FR. LESTER: *You* are — why?

FR. CULLEN: The students are walking around the campus with their shoes on. [Fr. Lester starts to windows]: Come look at them.

FR. LESTER: This I want to see — and don't they look nice!

FR. CULLEN: They certainly do.

FR. BROOKE: They didn't look too bad barefooted.

FR. CULLEN [Crossing back to center]: Now we can really settle down.

FR. LESTER: It may seem a little dull around here for a while.

FR. CULLEN: We don't have to worry about what's going to hit us next.

BR. THOMAS [starts out door and then calls back]: I wouldn't be too sure, Fathers — I wouldn't be *too* sure. [Exit]

[Singing is heard in the corridor.]

FR. LESTER: Now what's going on?

FR. CULLEN: If Brother Thomas starts anything . . .

[DUTCH JONES and the FOOTBALL TEAM troup in. They are still dressed in their tunics, and they are still barefooted, and they sing as they enter]

DUTCH: Father Brooke, we've come to tell you that we're leaving school.

FR. LESTER: You can't walk out in the middle of the semester—you'll lose your credits.

DUTCH: We won't need them, Father.

FR. CULLEN: Gorboduc Jones! You get a suit on and get back to class The Saint has gone.

DUTCH: We know, Father.

FR. CULLEN: Then get back to class.

DUTCH: We can't, Father.

FR. LESTER: Well, you can't go around looking like that. It's ridiculous. What will people think?

DUTCH: We don't care, Father. We're going to live the way the Saint taught us to.

[53]

FR. LESTER: But this is the 20th Century — you can't walk around in it barefooted! — Father Brooke, you say something to them.

FR. BROOKE: I can't think of a thing.

DUTCH: The Saint was barefooted.

FR. LESTER: But he's just *one* Saint. There are hundreds of others—why do you have to imitate him? What Saint Francis did was good and right for his time, but not for now. If you want to be a Saint, imitate a Doctor of the Church — imitate Aquinas, or de Sales, or somebody else who wore shoes.

FR. CULLEN: What's the matter with St. Ignatius? Why can't you imitate St. Ignatius?

DUTCH: St. Ignatius didn't come down and ask us, Father — Saint Francis did, and we couldn't refuse him after he came down and asked us.

FR. BROOKE: I can understand that.

FR. LESTER: But you can't do it this way — you can't just go marching off into Kansas — you don't even have a priest to say Mass!

DUTCH: Saint Francis said he'd send one.

FR. BROOKE: Did he say who?

DUTCH: No — he just said he'd found the right one for us.

FR. CULLEN: Where is he?

DUTCH: He'll come. — Goodbye, Fathers. — Let's go, Fellows — Brothers.

[The boys start out, singing softly, and then as they get farther away the volume rises.]

FR. LESTER: Somehow, Gorboduc Jones doesn't seem like the boy to found a new Order.

FR. CULLEN: He certainly doesn't.

FR. BROOKE: I agree with you. And he isn't going to. [they look at him] Gorboduc isn't going to found the new Order — I am. [he has walked center and dropped his shoes, with the socks inside, in the middle of the floor.]

FR. LESTER: You! Phil!

FR. CULLEN: Philip Brooke!   (simultaneously)

FR. LESTER: You can't found a new Order! You're a . . .

FR. BROOKE: Yes, I can. [crosses to door] I can if I can catch up with it. [dashes out calling] Hey, Friars, wait for me!

FR. CULLEN: If I hadn't seen it, I wouldn't believe — on second thought — on second thought —

[PHONE RINGS]

[54]

FR. LESTER [crossing to answer phone]: Thinking back quickly I can see a whole lot now . . . [answers phone] Hello. Hello. — Who? [to Father Cullen] It's Father Eddy, the president. — Yes, Eddy. — Did you have a good retreat? — You will? Fine. — Oh, yes, lots has happened, lots. You're going to be surprised. — All right. — Goodbye. [to Father Cullen] He and Jim are on their way home.

FR. CULLEN: That's good.

[There is a silence and Father Cullen walks to the windows and looks out.]

FR. LESTER [straightens desk up a little and sets check in prominent position where it can be seen immediately — he talks to himself]: Yes. They're going to be surprised [He chuckles to himself and then crosses to the windows and stands beside Father Cullen.]

FR. CULLEN: Look — there they go — singing — the "joyous minstrels of God."

FR. LESTER: Phil is up with them. — The way he catches cold, how long do you think he'll be able to say Mass barefooted?

FR. CULLEN: When he gets used to it he'll be all right.

FR. LESTER: But he'll sure miss a lot of Masses until he does get used to it. He catches cold when he takes off his shoes on Good Friday.

FR. CULLEN [facing him squarely]: Are you suggesting that he'll need some help?

FR. LESTER: Yes, I am.

FR. CULLEN: Well, don't just stand there talking — get going.

FR. LESTER: O.K.

[Father Lester sits in chair on one side of the stage and Father Cullen on the other. Both remove shoes and socks and put socks inside shoes. Father Lester places his shoes on one side of Father Brooke's and Father Cullen places his on the other side, so the three pairs are in a row, center stage.]

FR. LESTER: Come on — hurry. — We'll look like fools running after them.

[Father Cullen laughs.]

FR. LESTER: What are you laughing at?

FR. CULLEN: I was just thinking: there have been a lot of fools in the Church — we're in good company. — Let's go.

[They exit, and the lights fade, all except one spot on the three pairs of shoes.]

CURTAIN

Seven Nuns At Las Vegas

BY

Natalie E. White

Farce; modern; 2 acts; one interior set; 11 women and 2 men (can be done with one man)

Written at the request of William J. Elsen, Head of the Department of Speech, University of Notre Dame, for production by the nuns at the 1954 Notre Dame Summer Session, this farce has since been successfully performed by schools and colleges all over the country.

"The highly imaginative plot revolves around the experiences of seven nuns who, convent and all, during a snowy cold day in Indiana were transported to Las Vegas, Nevada. The effect of the presence of these good women in the environs of the temple of light living and general gaiety is amusingly written."
—Lib Wiley, *The Lynchburgh News*

"While the play is a farce, the nuns are not farcial characters nor are they characters of saccharine pietistic tendencies. They are rather the ordinary, gracious, efficient American nuns. The play technically is "well made," not carelessly constructed as plays about religion too frequently are. Miss White, an experienced playwright and teacher of playwriting, writes with the integrity of her profession."
—Sister M. Agnese, S.P., *Catholic Theatre*

"We highly recommend this play and are confident it will answer quests for a play that is both humorous and charming."
—*The Catholic Alumnae Quarterly*

"A play that has lilt and bounce from the first curtain to the last . . . . high quality." —Edward Fischer, *The Ave Maria*

DRAMATISTS PLAY SERVICE, INC.

14 East 38th Street

New York 16, N. Y.